LISTENER'S

Reflections

Reflections

*I*n today's world, the pace of life can be breathless and punishing, so it is important to find the time for peace and reflection. Classical music can play an invaluable role in fulfilling this universal need. J. S. Bach, Schubert, Schumann, Tchaikovsky, Verdi, Mahler, Fauré—these are just some of the great composers that are represented in this selection. Their music, whether for the orchestra, the piano, or voices can be guaranteed to soothe the mind and delight the spirit.

THE LISTENER'S GUIDE – WHAT THE SYMBOLS MEAN

THE COMPOSERS
Their lives... their loves..
their legacies...

THE MUSIC
Explanation... analysis...
interpretation...

THE INSPIRATION
How works of genius
came to be written

THE BACKGROUND
People, places, and events
linked to the music

© MCMXCVI IMP AB In Classical Mood™ IMP AB, produced under license by IMP Inc. Printed in China. US P 2201 11 002

Contents

– 2 –
Suite No.3 in D Major BWV 1068: Second Movement (Air)
JOHANN SEBASTIAN BACH

– 4 –
Piano Quintet in A Major D667, "The Trout": Second Movement
FRANZ SCHUBERT

– 6 –
Piano Concerto No.1 in B-flat Minor, Opus 23: Second Movement
PYOTR TCHAIKOVSKY

– 8 –
Carnival of the Animals: The Swan
CAMILLE SAINT-SAËNS

– 9 –
Appalachian Spring: Prelude
AARON COPLAND

– 10 –
Symphony No.5 in C-sharp Minor: Fourth Movement (Adagietto)
GUSTAV MAHLER

– 13 –
Trumpet Concerto in E-flat: Second Movement
JOSEPH HAYDN

– 14 –
The Marriage of Figaro K492: Aria ("Porgi amor")
WOLFGANG AMADEUS MOZART

– 16 –
Gymnopédie No.3
ERIK SATIE

– 18 –
Scenes from Childhood: Träumerei (Dreaming)
ROBERT SCHUMANN

– 19 –
Nabucco: Chorus of Hebrew Slaves ("Va, pensiero")
GIUSEPPE VERDI

– 20 –
Violin Concerto in D Major, Opus 77: Second Movement
JOHANNES BRAHMS

– 22 –
Serse: Largo
GEORGE FRIDERIC HANDEL

– 24 –
Requiem, Opus 48: Sanctus
GABRIEL FAURÉ

Suite No. 3 in D Major BWV 1068: Second Movement (Air)

Johann Sebastian Bach *1685–1750*

Suite No. 3 in D Major

BWV 1068: Second Movement (Air)

From the very first long, quiet note on the violins, this marvelous "air," or melody, induces a calm, contemplative state of mind. To the stately progress of the accompanying lower strings, the melody unfolds in an unbroken line right up to the final bar—all at the same unhurried pace. With music of such serene beauty, the cares of the world simply drift away, giving the soul and spirit time to breathe.

Air on the G String

This much-loved piece of music is widely known as the "Air on the G String". But it was not composed as such by Bach. He wrote it—as we hear it now—as a movement from his orchestral *Suite No.3*. It was well more than a century later that a fellow German, violinist August Wilhelmj, arranged the piece for violin and piano to be played on the G string of the violin because he thought it sounded better that way. Hence the popular title.

Suite No.3 in D Major BWV 1068: Second Movement (Air)

The Significance of the Suite

Suite means a "following" in the sense of a succession of individual pieces or movements. In the kind of suites that Bach composed, these movements were often modeled on old, courtly dances, such as the gavotte, gigue, and minuet. Such suites of the late Baroque age (in a musical context, Bach's period) helped to pave the way for the sonatas and symphonies of the succeeding Viennese Classical period (roughly 1750–1800). Incidentally, the term "Classical music" is restricted by musicologists to this late 18th-century music (notably the works of Haydn, Mozart, and the younger Beethoven), although, of course, it has come into general usage to describe all concert music.

Society Music

Bach wrote four orchestral suites. *Suite No.3* was composed some time after he had taken up the post, in 1723, as Cantor or Musical Director of the Church School of St. Thomas in Leipzig. He probably wrote it for a *collegium musicum* concert. This Latin title was once widely used to describe organized local music societies. Their concerts were often held at the home of a rich patron, or sometimes in the fashionable coffeehouses that sprang up everywhere during Bach's lifetime.

Key Notes

The violin has four strings, usually tuned to G, D, A, and E. But they can be tuned differently, either by tightening them to raise the pitch or loosening them to lower the pitch.

Piano Quintet in A Major
D667, "The Trout": Second Movement

Franz Schubert *1797–1828*

It is quite possible to be in a relaxed and reflective frame of mind without drifting off into a daydream. This lovely piece, marked *andante* ("at a steady, walking pace"), is sunny and bright in mood, and even quite animated in its middle section, especially in the piano part. At the same time, its obviously good-natured spirit reflects a mind freed from care or anxiety and able to look with tranquility and kindness upon the world.

Keeping Track of Schubert

Just as Mozart's compositions were catalogued by Ludwig Köchel (the K numbers), so another Austrian scholar, Dr. Otto Deutsch, produced a catalogue of all of Schubert's works. So each Schubert composition has its D number. There are well more than 900 individual works listed—from songs to symphonies. This was a phenomenal output for a composer who died at the tragically early age of 31.

Piano Quintet in A Major D667, "The Trout": Second Movement

Why "Trout"?

This movement has nothing specifically to do with fish or with water. The Fourth Movement, however, is based on the tune of an existing Schubert song called *The Trout*. So the quintet as a whole has come to be known by that name.

Songs such as *The Trout* were often first heard at happy gatherings of Schubert's friends. These occasions, known as "Schubertiads," made him very popular, but they did not earn him very much money.

The composer delighted his many friends with informal "Schubertiads," musical evenings during which many of his famous songs were performed for the first time.

An Unusual Lineup

The piano quintet was a popular type of chamber music composition during the 19th century. In most cases, the instrumental lineup is a string quartet (two violins, viola, cello) and piano. Schubert's *Trout* Quintet is different. This was written for violin, viola, cello, double bass, and piano. The inclusion of the bass gives the music a generally darker, richer sound.

Key Notes

Schubert's String Quartet in D Minor (D810) is known as the Death and the Maiden Quartet because, as with the Trout *Quintet*, one of its movements is based on a Schubert song with the same title.

Piano Concerto No. 1 in B-flat Minor, Opus 23: Second Movement

Pyotr Tchaikovsky *1840–1893*

Piano Concerto No. 1 in B-flat Minor

Opus 23: Second Movement

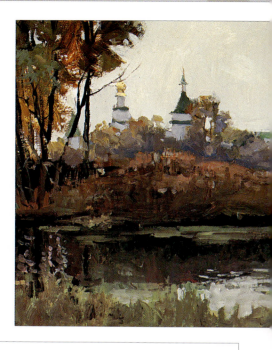

Flute, oboe, clarinets, horn, and cello step forward one by one to share the spotlight with the solo piano in this most delicate and enchanting of concerto movements. There is a much faster middle section, based on the tune of an old French folk song, which seems to come and go like an episode from a happy dream. But its light and mercurial character hardly disturbs the movement's prevailing mood of tender reflection.

With dynamic movements on either side, the tranquil Second Movement lies like a still pool.

Plucking the Strings

The solo flute at the opening of this movement of the First Piano Concerto is accompanied by the stringed instruments, played *pizzicato*. This Italian word ("pinched") instructs the players to pluck the strings instead of sounding them with the bow. Tchaikovsky also instructs the strings to be played with a mute (*con sordini*). This is a small clamp that is placed over the strings to soften their sound.

PIANO CONCERTO NO.1 IN B-FLAT MINOR, OPUS 23: SECOND MOVEMENT

A CLASH OF OPINIONS

The grand opening of Tchaikovsky's First Piano Concerto, with its big theme on the orchestra and leaping chords for the piano, makes it the most famous of all concertos. But Tchaikovsky's colleague at the Moscow Conservatory, Nicholai Rubinstein, thought it was all just terrible noise when the composer first played the music for him. Rubinstein, one of the finest pianists of his day, refused to give the work its first performance. That honor fell to the German pianist Hans von Bülow. He premiered the concerto not in Russia, but in Boston, Massachusetts, on October 25, 1875.

Nicholai Rubinstein (left) refused to give the concerto its premiere. Hans von Bülow (caricatured right) proved a fine substitute.

THE PATTERN OF REFUSAL

After his differences with Rubinstein over the First Piano Concerto, Tchaikovsky must have thought, "Here we go again!" when it came to his Violin Concerto. He dedicated that work to the Hungarian violinist Leopold Auer, a professor at the St. Petersburg Conservatory. But Auer said the music was unplayable and would not touch it. The first performance was then given by the Russian violinist Adolph Brodsky, this time in Vienna.

KEY NOTES

Tchaikovsky's Piano Concerto No.2 in G Major, Opus 44 also has some fiery and exciting music, but it never achieved the popularity and fame of the first.

CARNIVAL OF THE ANIMALS: THE SWAN

CAMILLE SAINT-SAËNS *1835–1921*

Carnival of the Animals

THE SWAN

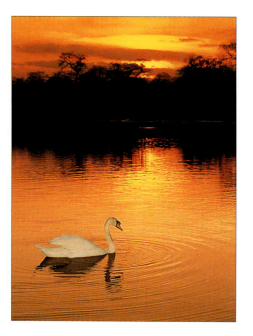

The mellow and noble tone of the cello and the graceful, dignified appearance of the swan make a perfect pair. Give to the cello one of its loveliest melodies, add a gently rippling piano accompaniment, and the picture is complete—of a swan gliding serenely over a peaceful stretch of river or a secluded lake. Here, too, are reflections in the water to mirror the calm reflections of the mind.

A PRIVATE JOKE

The French composer Saint-Saëns described his *Le Carnaval des Animaux* as a "grand zoological fantasy." For company, the swan has a donkey, a tortoise, an elephant, fish in an aquarium, hens and cocks, and a cuckoo. There are even some fossils. Saint-Saëns wrote the whole work primarily for his own enjoyment and banned its publication during his lifetime, in case it harmed his reputation as a serious composer. The one exception to this ban was "The Swan".

KEY NOTES

Another of Saint-Saëns' extremely popular pieces is his captivating "Wedding Cake Waltz" for piano and orchestra.

APPALACHIAN SPRING: PRELUDE

AARON COPLAND *1900–1990*

Appalachian Spring
PRELUDE

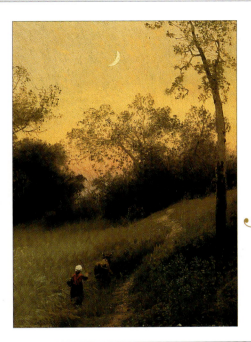

The soft, misty light of dawn can invite contemplation just as sweetly as dusk can. This is the mood that opens the ballet *Appalachian Spring*. Hushed string chords, with quiet calls on clarinets and flutes, trumpets, and horns, invoke the light of a new day stealing across the wooded valleys and slopes of the Appalachian Mountains. The characters then appear, one by one, ready for the day to begin.

BALLETS

Copland took the title *Appalachian Spring* from a poem by Hart Crane. The scenario, however, was devised by the renowned dancer and choreographer Martha Graham. It presents the simple yet touching story of a young farmer and his bride-to-be inspecting their newly built Pennsylvania farmhouse and meeting their neighbors. It creates a beautiful picture of the pioneering days of America. Two other ballets by Copland, *Billy the Kid* and *Rodeo*, were inspired by the old Wild West.

KEY NOTES

Copland won many awards, including a Pulitzer Prize for music in 1944, the year he composed Appalachian Spring.

Symphony No. 5 in C-sharp Minor: Fourth Movement (Adagietto)

Gustav Mahler *1860–1911*

Symphony No. 5 in C-sharp Minor

Fourth Movement (Adagietto)

In 1901, the 41-year-old Mahler met the pretty young music student Alma Schindler, and they were married the following year. He was working on his Fifth Symphony at the time, and this *adagietto* movement can be heard as his declaration of love for Alma. Scored for just strings and harp, it unfolds with one of the composer's sweetest melodies. The music also seems to progress like a series of deep breaths, rising to one great yearning sigh, before subsiding again at the very end. This is a deeply reflective interlude in an otherwise stormy and dramatic symphony that simply bursts with the exhilaration of life.

All about Adagietto

The Italian word *adagio* describes music to be played at a slow pace or tempo. *Adagietto,* or "little *adagio,*" indicates a tempo not quite so slow as in a true *adagio*. The term *adagietto* can also describe a piece of music that is both fairly slow and fairly brief in duration. It carries both meanings in this symphonic movement.

Symphony No.5 in C-sharp Minor: Fourth Movement (Adagietto)

Death in Venice

This haunting music was used to memorable effect in the movie *Death in Venice*, about a doomed composer dying of cholera. In the original novel by the German writer Thomas Mann, the central character is another writer, not a composer. However, Mann gave his fictional creation both the physical characteristics of Mahler and the first name Gustav.

The movie Death in Venice *created an indelible association between Mahler's music and that city.*

Joy and Sorrow

The middle-aged Mahler might have thought that the prospect of family life had passed him by when he met and married Alma. He was certainly overjoyed when she bore him two children. But tragedy soon struck. The elder child died from diphtheria. Then Mahler himself was told he had an incurable heart condition. His unrelenting workload no doubt hastened his own death at the age of 51. The widowed Alma later married the famous German architect Walter Gropius.

SYMPHONY NO. 5 IN C-SHARP MINOR: FOURTH MOVEMENT (ADAGIETTO)

Maestro Mahler

Mahler's huge and complex symphonies are very popular all over the world today. In his own lifetime, however, Mahler was far better known as a conductor. As musical director at the prestigious Vienna Court Opera, he revolutionized everything—the playing of the orchestra, the singing and acting of the cast, and stage and costume design. From Vienna, Mahler moved to New York, to conduct both at the Metropolitan Opera and the New York Philharmonic Orchestra. The image of the conductor as a highly respected figure began with him.

Mahler was celebrated as a conductor on both sides of the Atlantic.

Inescapable Fate

It is said that Mahler was afraid of writing a ninth symphony because Beethoven, Schubert, Bruckner, and Dvořák had not gotten beyond that fateful number. To forestall events, Mahler turned what might have been his ninth symphony into an orchestral song cycle, *The Song of the Earth*. Then he went on to write his actual *Symphony No. 9*—and died soon afterward while working on a 10th!

Key Notes

The Fifth Symphony was not written sequentially. Mahler began with the pivotal Third Movement, then added the first two, and finally, the Adagietto and the Fifth.

TRUMPET CONCERTO IN E-FLAT: SECOND MOVEMENT

JOSEPH HAYDN *1732–1809*

Trumpet Concerto in E-flat

SECOND MOVEMENT

Haydn wrote this concerto in 1796, having recently returned home to Vienna after two triumphant visits to England. At the age of 64, he was the most revered living composer. Perhaps Haydn was looking back contentedly over his mostly happy and illustrious life as he wrote this restful movement. Certainly the trumpet, which can sound very piercing and imperious, here takes on a warm and mellow tone.

KEY NOTES

Haydn's is one of two famous trumpet concertos of the Classical period—the other was written by his contemporary, Johann Hummel.

INSTRUMENTAL DEVELOPMENT

Compared with the piano or the violin, there are very few concertos for the trumpet. Haydn wrote this one for the Viennese court trupeter Anton Weidinger, who had recently pioneered an instrument with keys. The old, "natural" trumpets, consisting simply of a long, straight tube, could only sound a limited number of notes. Keyed trumpets were replaced by the valve trumpets of today.

THE MARRIAGE OF FIGARO K492: ARIA ("PORGI AMOR")

WOLFGANG AMADEUS MOZART *1756–1791*

The Marriage of Figaro
K492, ARIA ("PORGI AMOR")

Act II of the opera opens with this beautiful, soulful aria sung by the Countess Almaviva. Her husband the Count is a philanderer who has his eye on his wife's maid, Susanna. Sadly, the Countess remembers the love that the Count once felt for her. "Porgi amor..." ("Oh love, bring some relief") she sings, to one of Mozart's simplest but most heartfelt melodies, calling on the spirit of love to turn her husband's affections back to her. It is a passage of exquisite tenderness in this greatest of comic masterpieces.

THE MAGNIFICENT TRIO

After the success of *The Marriage of Figaro* in 1786, Mozart and his brilliant librettist, Lorenzo da Ponte, wrote two more wonderful operas together. In the following year came *Don Giovanni*, based on the life of the legendary Don Juan, and in 1790, *Cosi fan tutte*, a rather cynical title about romantic love that means "They're all the same!"

The Marriage of Figaro K492: Aria ("Porgi Amor")

Beaumarchais's play The Marriage of Figaro *was one of the sparks that kindled the French Revolution.*

Opera Revolution

The Marriage of Figaro is in the style Italian *opera buffa*—comic opera. But it is far more than comedy. Mozart's librettist, Lorenzo da Ponte, based his scenario on a play by French dramatist Pierre Beaumarchais, which attacked the aristocracy and critically influenced opinion as France moved toward revolution. The opera is not as inflammatory, but it still sides with the manservant, Figaro, against his master, Count Almaviva. As Figaro declares, "One day, the Count will dance to my tune!"

The Birth of the Clarinet

The orchestral accompaniment to Countess Almaviva's aria has some prominent parts for the clarinets, among other woodwind instruments. The clarinet was a relatively new instrument in Mozart's day, and he was the first major composer to write extensively for it. The playing of the Viennese court musician Anton Stadler did much to inspire him. In fact, the type of clarinet Stadler often played was the curiously named basset horn, which could sound deeper notes than the modern clarinet. Mozart loved the sound of it.

The 18th-century basset horn

Key Notes

Thirty years after Mozart and da Ponte wrote The Marriage of Figaro, *Rossini composed his comic masterpiece,* The Barber of Seville. *This features some of the same characters as Mozart's opera, including Figaro (as the barber) and Count Almaviva, but at an earlier time in their lives.*

GYMNOPÉDIE NO. 3

ERIK SATIE *1866–1925 (Orchestrated by Claude Debussy)*

Gymnopédie No.3

The French title *Gymnopédie* refers to the choruses and dances performed in ancient Greece in honor of Apollo, the sun god who also inspired music and poetry. The slow, deliberate, and quite hypnotic pace and sound of this piece marvelously captures the solemn and mysterious mood of these ritual dances. Such music also invites us to cast our minds back to a time and place strangely different from our own.

GYMNOPÉDIE NO.3

FRENCH REVOLUTION

Satie led a revolt against the strong influence of Wagner and other German composers on French music in the early years of the 20th century. "Music without sauerkraut!" was his cry. To escape from this "Teutonic seriousness," Satie wrote pieces of music with such silly titles as *Three Pieces in the Shape of a Pear* and *Limp Preludes for a Dog*! Satie also wrote the music to a ballet, *Parade*, with scenery and costumes designed by Pablo Picasso. A critic described the work as "surreal," coining the term "Surrealism" to describe artistic creation that explores the world of dreams and of the subconscious mind.

Satie's music for Parade *was adapted to feed the latest popular music craze—syncopated ragtime.*

A STRANGE BIRD

Satie was a great eccentric and extremely anti-establishment. At one point in his life, he was a member of the mysterious Rosicrucians, a spiritual group that explored white magic and alchemy. He even wrote some strange music for their ceremonies. Satie then formed his own church, excommunicating anyone who disagreed with him!

KEY NOTES

Satie wrote Gymnopédie No.3 for solo piano. His friend Claude Debussy thought highly of the piece and offered to orchestrate it. This is the form in which it has remained so popular.

SCENES FROM CHILDHOOD: TRÄUMEREI (DREAMING)

ROBERT SCHUMANN *1810–1856*

Scenes from Childhood

TRÄUMEREI (DREAMING)

Träumerei is German for "reverie," and the mood of relaxed and happy daydreaming created by this much-loved piece can be shared by everyone, young and old. If there is a moment of doubt or anxiety in the middle section, it just as swiftly passes, the music moving to a hushed and blissful close, and lingering fondly in the mind long after the final chord has died away.

THROUGH THE EYES OF A CHILD

With his group of piano pieces called *Kinderscenen (Scenes from Childhood)*, Schumann was one of the first composers to take childhood as a theme, re-creating in music the child's sense of wonder. This is music written by an adult about childhood, not music written exclusively for children. Other composers, notably Mussorgsky with his song cycle *The Nursery*, and Debussy with his *Children's Corner Suite*, followed Schumann down this fascinating musical path.

KEY NOTES

Schumann also wrote Album for the Young, a larger group of relatively simple piano pieces for children to learn and play. "The Happy Peasant" is a well-known piece from this collection.

Nabucco: Chorus of Hebrew Slaves ("Va, pensiero")

Giuseppe Verdi *1813–1901*

Nabucco

Chorus of Hebrew Slaves ("Va, pensiero")

Nabucco is Italian for Nebuchadnezzar, the king of ancient Babylon, who, as recounted in the Old Testament of the Bible, conquered Judah and enslaved the Children of Israel. In Verdi's opera, Hebrew slaves gather by the banks of the river Euphrates to lament upon their present sad fate. "Va, pensiero" means "Fly, thought," and, as their voices rise above the orchestra, the slaves fondly recall the psalms they sang in their beloved homeland of Israel and find renewed hope in their eventual liberation.

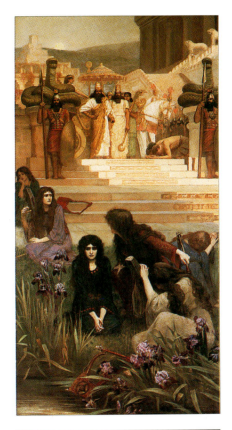

Verdi's Breakthrough

Nabucco was a sensation when it opened in Milan in 1842. In the plight of the Israelites, the Italian audience saw echoes of their own situation under Austrian domination. At Verdi's funeral in 1901, a huge throng burst into the song that had come to symbolize Italian freedom, "Va, pensiero."

Key Notes

At the premiere of *Nabucco*, Verdi, who had recently lost both his wife and young son, met the singer Giuseppina Strepponi, who became his second wife.

Violin Concerto in D Major, Opus 77: Second Movement

Johannes Brahms *1833–1897*

Violin Concerto in D Major
Opus 77: Second Movement

Brahms introduces the beautiful main theme of this movement on the wind instruments of the orchestra (horns, bassoons, clarinets, oboes, flutes), making them sound as gentle and beguiling as the violin itself. When the solo violin does add its own expressive voice, the music becomes as radiant as a calm and cloudless sky.

A Singular Composition

When Beethoven wrote his one and only violin concerto, he set a precedent for many other great composers who came after him. Brahms, Dvořák, Tchaikovsky, Sibelius, and Elgar each wrote only one violin concerto. Perhaps they felt that if one such work was good enough for Beethoven, then it was surely good enough for them!

Violin Concerto in D Major, Opus 77: Second Movement

The Hungarian Connection

The violinist Joseph Joachim and one of his fellow Hungarian pupils, Eduard Remenyi, first interested the serious-minded Brahms in the colorful folk music of their native land. Their own compositions were often infused with the high spirits of gypsy music. And we have them to thank for the composer's ever-popular *Hungarian Dances*, as well as for the fiery last movement of this marvelous violin concerto.

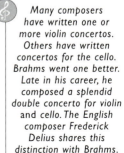

Joseph Joachim (right) *interested his friend Brahms in the exciting rhythms of Hungarian folk music.*

Virtuoso Friendship

Brahms wrote his violin concerto in collaboration with his long-time friend, the virtuoso Joseph Joachim. He asked Joachim to correct any awkward or impractical passages in the solo part. Joachim also wrote out a splendid *cadenza* (a section of the score in a concerto reserved for the soloist alone) for the big first movement. And it was Joachim who gave the first performance of the work in Leipzig, Germany, on New Year's Day, 1879.

Key Notes

Many composers have written one or more violin concertos. Others have written concertos for the cello. Brahms went one better. Late in his career, he composed a splendid double concerto for violin and cello. The English composer Frederick Delius shares this distinction with Brahms.

Serse: Largo

George Frideric Handel
1685–1759

Serse

LARGO

Largo is the Italian name for a piece of music played at a dignified pace. Handel's much-loved "Largo" is, in fact, an instrumental arrangement of an aria from his opera *Serse* (or *Xerxes*). The ancient Persian king of the title falls in love with his brother's fiancée, and he is ridden with guilt. But in this aria, he finds momentary peace beneath the cool shade of a tree. The beautiful, stately melody perfectly suggests a refuge from the burning heat of the sun that calms the restless spirit.

Opera Seria

The operas Handel wrote are called *opera seria*—serious opera. They were based on a handful of tales from ancient history. The stories were almost always about a struggle, on the part of the hero or heroine, between love and duty. *Opera seria* was full of strict rules about what kinds of voices should sing each role and how many arias each singer should have. Despite such restrictions, Handel kept his operas fresh and alive with such glorious music as his "Largo".

SERSE: LARGO

THE KING OF OPERA

Although Handel was not primarily a composer of religious music, his oratorio, *Messiah*, is one of the world's most popular works. Born in Germany, he settled in London and made his fortune writing operas for the commercial theater. When his kind of opera began to go out of fashion, Handel turned to writing *oratorios*—similar in style to operas, but not staged, and usually based on a story from the Bible. They proved very lucrative for him.

Right: *A modern production of Handel's* Julius Caesar, *with contralto Dame Janet Baker in the role of Caesar.*

A MAN OF HIS TIME

The world of opera in 18th-century London was a cutthroat business. Fortunes were made and lost overnight, but Handel was more than able to take care of his own interests. There is a famous story about the way he dealt with one real-life "prima donna" who insisted on singing an aria her way, not his. He grabbed hold of her and dangled her from out of an upstairs window, roaring that, while she might be a devil, he was Satan himself!

KEY NOTES

In a modern production of Serse, *the part of the male hero is actually sung by a female contralto. In Handel's time, it would have been sung by a castrato—a mature male whose youthful high voice had been preserved by castrating him before puberty. Castrati were the singing superstars of their time, commanding huge fees.*

Requiem, Opus 48: Sanctus

Gabriel Fauré
1845-1924

Requiem
Opus 48: Sanctus

After a brief, hushed introduction on violas, organ, and harp, the voices enter. First come sopranos, then tenors and basses, intoning the word *sanctus* to the same gentle phrase. Horns and trumpet later reinforce the words of the choir, before the movement dies quietly away. The listener does not need to be especially religious to fall in with the mood of spiritual calm and joy that pervades this sublime music.

Lengthy Revision

For a work of such tranquility, Fauré's *Requiem* had quite a troublesome birth. The composer wrote the earliest part of it in 1877. He went on to complete the first version in 1888, moved by the recent deaths of his father and mother. Fauré made many more revisions before the final version was published in 1901.

Requiem, Opus 48: Sanctus

The Composer as Organist

Fauré followed a long and honorable tradition among French composers of serving as organist at one of the big Paris churches. In his case, it was at the fashionable and prestigious church of the Madeleine, where Saint-Saëns had been organist before him. Ironically, Fauré was not a particularly religious man. He much preferred writing songs and piano music—which makes his beautiful *Requiem* all the more remarkable.

As well as composing, Fauré (above) enjoyed a distinguished career as an organist, notably in the magnificent church of the Madeleine (right).

A Tranquil Setting

The Latin term *requiem aeternam* means "eternal rest," and the Roman Catholic *Requiem Mass* is said or sung in memory of the dead. Many composers, including Palestrina, Mozart, Berlioz, and Verdi, have set parts or all of the mass text to music. The most dramatic section is the "Dies Irae" ("Day of Wrath"), with its awesome sounding of the *tuba mirum*—the Last Trumpet—calling the dead to account. Significantly, Fauré omits the "Dies Irae", and for many people, his is the most peaceful and the loveliest of all settings of the *Requiem*.

Key Notes

In his later years, Fauré grew increasingly hard of hearing, and for this reason, he resigned as Director of the Paris Conservatoire. But he managed to keep his deafness a secret from all but his closest friends until the day he died.

Credits & Acknowledgments

Picture Credits

Cover / Title page / IBC: **Images Colour Library**

AKG: 12(tr), 21(c), 23 (c); **AKG** / E. Lessing: 5(tr), 10; **C. Barda / PAL**: 23 (tr); **Bridgeman Art Library/** Private Collection 2 (tr); Museo Correr, Venice/Giraudon 3(cr); Roy Miles Gallery, London 6 -7; Agnew and Sons, London 14; Royal Holloway and Bedford New College, London 18(tl); Christie's, London 19(r); Church of St Peter and St Paul, Cattistock 24; **J.L.Charmet**: 25(b); **Christie's Images**: 9(tl); Bruce Coleman/Pott: 13; **E.T. Archive**: 15(tl), (cl); **Mary Evans Picture Library**: 17(c), 21(tr); **Hulton Deutsch Collection**: 7(r); 25(cl); **Images Colour Library**: 11(tr); **Lebrecht Collection**: 7(cl), 11(br,) 12 (cl); **Private Collection**: 17(tr); **Sotheby's Transparency Library**: 3(tl), 16; **Tate Gallery London**: 22; **Tony Stone Images** / R.Talbot: 4; P.Ingrand 8; **ZEFA**/Eckstein: 20.

Artwork & Symbols: John See